50 Italy Spoon Dishes

By: Kelly Johnson

Table of Contents

- Risotto
- Minestrone
- Zuppa di Fagioli (Bean Soup)
- Ribollita
- Stracciatella Soup
- Pasta e Fagioli
- Zuppa Toscana
- Polenta
- Vellutata (Velvety Soup)
- Pappa al Pomodoro
- Gnocchi alla Sorrentina
- Lasagna alla Bolognese
- Cannelloni
- Tortellini in Brodo
- Brodo di Carne (Meat Broth)
- Zuppa di Pesce (Fish Soup)
- Minestra Maritata
- Pastiera Napoletana
- Cacciucco
- Sanguinaccio
- Frittata di Patate
- Zuppa di Porri (Leek Soup)
- Zuppa di Cavolo Nero (Kale Soup)
- Risotto alla Milanese
- Risotto ai Funghi (Mushroom Risotto)
- Risotto alla Pescatora (Seafood Risotto)
- Risotto alla Carbonara
- Risotto al Nero di Seppia (Squid Ink Risotto)
- Zuppa di Cipolle (Onion Soup)
- Zuppa di Asparagi (Asparagus Soup)
- Crema di Pomodoro (Tomato Cream Soup)
- Sformato di Melanzane (Eggplant Flan)
- Purè di Patate (Mashed Potatoes)
- Trippa alla Romana
- Polenta con Funghi

- Polenta con Cinghiale (Polenta with Wild Boar)
- Fagioli all'Uccelletto
- Parmigiana di Melanzane (Eggplant Parmesan)
- Gnocchi alla Romana
- Risotto al Gorgonzola
- Tortino di Riso (Rice Cake)
- Pasticcio di Carne
- Insalata Caprese (Caprese Salad)
- Cannoli Siciliani (Sicilian Pastry)
- Tiramisu
- Panna Cotta
- Cassata Siciliana
- Sformato di Ricotta (Ricotta Flan)
- Zuppa di Zucca (Pumpkin Soup)
- Focaccia al Rosmarino (Rosemary Focaccia)

Risotto

Ingredients:

- 1 cup Arborio rice
- 4 cups chicken or vegetable broth
- 1 small onion, chopped
- 2 tbsp butter
- 1 tbsp olive oil
- 1/2 cup dry white wine
- 1/2 cup grated Parmesan cheese
- Salt and pepper to taste

Instructions: In a large saucepan, heat the broth and keep it warm over low heat. In a separate pan, heat the olive oil and butter. Add the chopped onion and sauté until soft. Add the rice to the pan and stir to coat with butter and oil, cooking for 1-2 minutes. Pour in the wine and cook until the liquid evaporates. Begin adding the warm broth, one ladle at a time, stirring constantly until the liquid is absorbed before adding more. Continue this process until the rice is tender (about 18-20 minutes). Stir in the Parmesan cheese, and season with salt and pepper. Serve hot and enjoy!

Minestrone

Ingredients:

- 1 onion, chopped
- 2 carrots, chopped
- 2 celery stalks, chopped
- 2 medium potatoes, peeled and cubed
- 1 zucchini, chopped
- 1 cup green beans, chopped
- 1 cup canned tomatoes, crushed
- 4 cups vegetable broth
- 1 cup pasta (small shapes like ditalini or elbow macaroni)
- 1 can cannellini beans, drained and rinsed
- 2 tbsp olive oil
- Salt and pepper to taste
- Fresh basil for garnish

Instructions: In a large pot, heat the olive oil over medium heat. Add the onion, carrots, celery, and potatoes. Cook for about 5 minutes, stirring occasionally. Add the zucchini, green beans, and crushed tomatoes. Stir well. Pour in the vegetable broth and bring the soup to a boil. Lower the heat and simmer for 20 minutes until the vegetables are tender. Add the pasta and cannellini beans and cook until the pasta is tender (about 10-12 minutes). Season with salt and pepper. Garnish with fresh basil and serve hot.

Zuppa di Fagioli (Bean Soup)

Ingredients:

- 1 onion, chopped
- 2 garlic cloves, minced
- 2 carrots, chopped
- 2 celery stalks, chopped
- 2 cans cannellini beans, drained and rinsed
- 4 cups vegetable broth
- 1/4 cup olive oil
- 1 tsp dried rosemary
- 1/2 tsp crushed red pepper flakes (optional)
- Salt and pepper to taste
- Fresh parsley, chopped (for garnish)

Instructions: Heat olive oil in a large pot over medium heat. Add the onion, garlic, carrots, and celery. Cook for about 7-10 minutes, until softened. Add the beans, vegetable broth, rosemary, and red pepper flakes. Bring to a boil. Lower the heat and simmer for 20 minutes, allowing the flavors to combine. Season with salt and pepper. Serve with a sprinkle of fresh parsley and a drizzle of olive oil.

Ribollita

Ingredients:

- 2 tbsp olive oil
- 1 onion, chopped
- 2 carrots, chopped
- 2 celery stalks, chopped
- 1 bunch kale, chopped
- 4 cups vegetable broth
- 2 cups stale bread, torn into pieces
- 2 cans cannellini beans, drained and rinsed
- 2 tbsp tomato paste
- 1/2 tsp dried thyme
- Salt and pepper to taste
- Fresh parsley for garnish

Instructions: Heat olive oil in a large pot over medium heat. Add the onion, carrots, and celery, cooking for 10 minutes until softened. Stir in the kale, vegetable broth, tomato paste, and thyme. Bring to a boil. Lower the heat and simmer for 15 minutes. Add the beans and stale bread, stirring to combine. Simmer for another 20 minutes until the bread breaks down and thickens the soup. Season with salt and pepper. Serve hot, garnished with fresh parsley.

Stracciatella Soup

Ingredients:

- 4 cups chicken broth
- 2 large eggs
- 1/4 cup grated Parmesan cheese
- 1 tbsp olive oil
- 1 tbsp chopped parsley
- Salt and pepper to taste

Instructions: Heat the chicken broth in a pot over medium heat until it is hot but not boiling. In a bowl, whisk the eggs with the Parmesan cheese. Slowly drizzle the egg mixture into the hot broth, stirring constantly to form delicate ribbons. Stir in the olive oil and parsley. Season with salt and pepper, then serve immediately.

Pasta e Fagioli

Ingredients:

- 1 onion, chopped
- 2 carrots, chopped
- 2 celery stalks, chopped
- 2 garlic cloves, minced
- 1 can cannellini beans, drained and rinsed
- 1 can diced tomatoes
- 4 cups vegetable broth
- 1 cup small pasta (ditalini or elbow)
- 2 tbsp olive oil
- 1 tsp dried oregano
- Salt and pepper to taste
- Fresh basil, chopped for garnish

Instructions: Heat olive oil in a large pot over medium heat. Add the onion, carrots, celery, and garlic. Sauté for 8-10 minutes until softened. Stir in the beans, tomatoes, and vegetable broth. Bring to a boil. Lower the heat and simmer for 20 minutes. Add the pasta and cook until al dente, about 10 minutes. Season with oregano, salt, and pepper. Serve garnished with fresh basil.

Zuppa Toscana

Ingredients:

- 1 lb Italian sausage
- 4 cups chicken broth
- 1 cup heavy cream
- 4 large potatoes, sliced thin
- 2 cups kale, chopped
- 2 garlic cloves, minced
- Salt and pepper to taste

Instructions: In a large pot, cook the sausage over medium heat until browned. Drain excess fat. Add the garlic and cook for another minute. Pour in the chicken broth and bring to a simmer. Add the potatoes and cook until tender, about 15 minutes. Stir in the kale and heavy cream. Cook for another 5 minutes. Season with salt and pepper, and serve hot.

Polenta

Ingredients:

- 1 cup polenta (cornmeal)
- 4 cups water or broth
- 2 tbsp butter
- 1/2 cup grated Parmesan cheese
- Salt to taste

Instructions: In a pot, bring the water or broth to a boil. Slowly whisk in the polenta. Reduce the heat to low and cook, stirring frequently for 25-30 minutes until thickened. Stir in the butter and Parmesan cheese. Season with salt and serve hot.

Vellutata (Velvety Soup)

Ingredients:

- 2 tbsp olive oil
- 1 onion, chopped
- 2 potatoes, peeled and chopped
- 2 cups cauliflower florets
- 4 cups vegetable broth
- 1/2 cup heavy cream
- Salt and pepper to taste

Instructions: Heat olive oil in a pot over medium heat. Add the onion and sauté for 5 minutes until soft. Add the potatoes and cauliflower, and stir for another 5 minutes. Pour in the vegetable broth and bring to a simmer. Cook until the vegetables are tender, about 20 minutes. Use an immersion blender or regular blender to puree the soup until smooth. Stir in the heavy cream, then season with salt and pepper. Serve hot.

Pappa al Pomodoro

Ingredients:

- 1 tbsp olive oil
- 1 onion, chopped
- 2 garlic cloves, minced
- 4 cups canned tomatoes, crushed
- 4 cups vegetable broth
- 4 cups stale bread, torn into pieces
- Salt and pepper to taste
- Fresh basil for garnish

Instructions: Heat olive oil in a large pot over medium heat. Add the onion and garlic and cook until softened, about 5 minutes. Add the crushed tomatoes and vegetable broth, bring to a simmer, and cook for 20 minutes. Stir in the bread and cook for another 15-20 minutes until the bread breaks down and the soup thickens. Season with salt and pepper. Serve hot, garnished with fresh basil.

Gnocchi alla Sorrentina

Ingredients:

- 1 lb gnocchi
- 2 cups marinara sauce
- 1 1/2 cups mozzarella cheese, shredded
- 1/4 cup grated Parmesan cheese
- 1 tbsp fresh basil, chopped
- Olive oil for greasing

Instructions: Preheat the oven to 375°F (190°C). Cook the gnocchi in salted boiling water until they float, about 2-3 minutes. Drain and place in a greased baking dish. Pour the marinara sauce over the gnocchi, then sprinkle with mozzarella and Parmesan cheese. Bake for 20 minutes, or until the cheese is melted and golden. Garnish with fresh basil and serve.

Lasagna alla Bolognese

Ingredients:

- 12 lasagna noodles
- 1 lb ground beef
- 1 onion, chopped
- 2 garlic cloves, minced
- 2 cups Bolognese sauce (beef, tomatoes, onions, carrots, celery)
- 2 cups ricotta cheese
- 2 cups mozzarella cheese, shredded
- 1/4 cup grated Parmesan cheese
- Salt and pepper to taste

Instructions: Preheat the oven to 375°F (190°C). Cook the lasagna noodles according to package instructions, then drain and set aside. In a pan, cook the ground beef, onion, and garlic until browned. Stir in the Bolognese sauce and simmer for 20 minutes. In a baking dish, layer the lasagna noodles, followed by ricotta cheese, Bolognese sauce, mozzarella, and Parmesan. Repeat the layers, finishing with a layer of cheese on top. Cover with foil and bake for 40 minutes, removing the foil during the last 10 minutes to allow the top to brown. Let it rest for 10 minutes before serving.

Cannelloni

Ingredients:

- 12 cannelloni tubes
- 2 cups ricotta cheese
- 1 cup spinach, cooked and chopped
- 1 egg
- 1 cup marinara sauce
- 1/2 cup grated Parmesan cheese
- Salt and pepper to taste

Instructions: Preheat the oven to 375°F (190°C). Cook the cannelloni tubes according to package instructions, then drain. In a bowl, combine the ricotta cheese, spinach, egg, salt, and pepper. Stuff the cannelloni tubes with the ricotta mixture. Spread a thin layer of marinara sauce in a baking dish and place the stuffed cannelloni on top. Pour the remaining marinara sauce over the cannelloni and sprinkle with Parmesan cheese. Cover with foil and bake for 30 minutes, removing the foil during the last 10 minutes to allow the top to brown.

Tortellini in Brodo

Ingredients:

- 1 lb fresh tortellini
- 6 cups chicken broth
- 1/2 cup Parmesan cheese, grated
- Salt and pepper to taste

Instructions: In a large pot, bring the chicken broth to a boil. Reduce the heat and add the tortellini, cooking according to package instructions (usually 2-3 minutes). Once cooked, ladle the tortellini and broth into bowls. Sprinkle with grated Parmesan cheese and season with salt and pepper. Serve hot.

Brodo di Carne (Meat Broth)

Ingredients:

- 1 lb beef stew meat
- 1 onion, peeled and halved
- 2 carrots, peeled and cut into chunks
- 2 celery stalks, cut into chunks
- 4 garlic cloves, smashed
- 10 cups water
- 1 bay leaf
- Salt and pepper to taste

Instructions: In a large pot, add the beef, onion, carrots, celery, garlic, and bay leaf. Pour in the water and bring to a boil. Reduce the heat and simmer for 2-3 hours, skimming the foam off the top as needed. Season with salt and pepper. Strain the broth and discard the solids. Serve hot as a base for soups or enjoy as a simple broth.

Zuppa di Pesce (Fish Soup)

Ingredients:

- 1 lb mixed fish (cod, shrimp, mussels, squid)
- 4 cups fish stock or water
- 1 onion, chopped
- 2 garlic cloves, minced
- 2 tbsp olive oil
- 1/2 cup white wine
- 1 can diced tomatoes
- 1/2 tsp dried oregano
- Salt and pepper to taste
- Fresh parsley, chopped (for garnish)

Instructions: In a large pot, heat the olive oil over medium heat. Add the onion and garlic and sauté for 5 minutes until softened. Add the white wine and cook for another minute. Stir in the tomatoes, fish stock, oregano, salt, and pepper. Bring to a boil, then reduce the heat and simmer for 20 minutes. Add the mixed fish and cook for 10-15 minutes, or until the fish is cooked through. Garnish with fresh parsley and serve hot.

Minestra Maritata

Ingredients:

- 1 lb sausage, removed from casings
- 1/2 lb escarole or kale, chopped
- 1 onion, chopped
- 2 garlic cloves, minced
- 4 cups chicken broth
- 1 cup white beans, cooked or canned
- 1 tbsp olive oil
- Salt and pepper to taste

Instructions: Heat olive oil in a large pot over medium heat. Add the sausage and cook, breaking it up into pieces, until browned. Add the onion and garlic and cook for 5 minutes until softened. Stir in the escarole, chicken broth, and white beans. Bring to a simmer and cook for 30 minutes, allowing the flavors to combine. Season with salt and pepper, then serve hot.

Pastiera Napoletana

Ingredients:

- 1 pie crust
- 1 1/2 cups ricotta cheese
- 1 cup cooked wheat berries
- 1/2 cup sugar
- 1/2 cup candied citrus peel, chopped
- 4 eggs
- 1/4 cup orange blossom water
- 1 tsp ground cinnamon

Instructions: Preheat the oven to 350°F (175°C). In a bowl, combine the ricotta cheese, cooked wheat berries, sugar, candied citrus peel, eggs, orange blossom water, and cinnamon. Mix until smooth. Pour the mixture into the pie crust. Bake for 45-50 minutes until the filling is set and golden on top. Let the pastiera cool completely before serving.

Cacciucco

Ingredients:

- 1 lb mixed seafood (octopus, squid, shrimp, fish)
- 4 cups fish stock or water
- 1 onion, chopped
- 2 garlic cloves, minced
- 2 tbsp olive oil
- 1/2 cup dry red wine
- 1 can diced tomatoes
- 1 tsp dried oregano
- Salt and pepper to taste
- 4 slices crusty bread

Instructions: In a large pot, heat the olive oil over medium heat. Add the onion and garlic and sauté until softened, about 5 minutes. Add the red wine and cook for another 2 minutes. Stir in the diced tomatoes, fish stock, oregano, salt, and pepper. Bring to a boil, then reduce to a simmer and cook for 20 minutes. Add the mixed seafood and cook for 10-15 minutes, until the seafood is cooked through. Toast the bread and serve with the soup, ladling the seafood and broth over the slices of bread.

Sanguinaccio

Ingredients:

- 1 1/2 cups pig's blood (available at butcher shops or specialty markets)
- 1 cup milk
- 1/2 cup sugar
- 1 tbsp cocoa powder
- 1 tbsp cinnamon
- 1/2 tsp vanilla extract
- 1 tbsp cornstarch
- 1 tbsp butter

Instructions: In a saucepan, combine the milk, sugar, cocoa powder, cinnamon, and vanilla extract. Bring to a simmer, stirring constantly. In a separate bowl, mix the pig's blood with the cornstarch to create a smooth slurry. Gradually add the blood mixture into the simmering milk mixture, stirring constantly. Continue to cook on low heat until it thickens to a creamy consistency. Stir in the butter for extra smoothness. Serve with bread or desserts.

Frittata di Patate (Potato Frittata)

Ingredients:

- 4 large potatoes, peeled and thinly sliced
- 8 eggs
- 1 onion, chopped
- 2 tbsp olive oil
- Salt and pepper to taste
- Fresh parsley for garnish

Instructions: In a large skillet, heat the olive oil over medium heat. Add the potatoes and onions and sauté until softened, about 10 minutes. In a separate bowl, whisk the eggs with salt and pepper. Once the potatoes are cooked, pour the eggs over the mixture in the skillet, ensuring it covers everything evenly. Cook on low heat for about 10-12 minutes, gently stirring occasionally to allow the eggs to set. Once the frittata is fully cooked, slide it onto a plate and garnish with fresh parsley. Serve warm or at room temperature.

Zuppa di Porri (Leek Soup)

Ingredients:

- 2 leeks, cleaned and chopped
- 1 onion, chopped
- 2 garlic cloves, minced
- 4 cups vegetable broth
- 2 medium potatoes, peeled and cubed
- 1 tbsp olive oil
- 1/2 cup cream (optional)
- Salt and pepper to taste

Instructions: In a large pot, heat olive oil over medium heat. Add the leeks, onion, and garlic and sauté for about 5 minutes, until softened. Add the potatoes and vegetable broth, bring to a boil, then reduce to a simmer. Cook for 20 minutes, or until the potatoes are tender. Use an immersion blender to puree the soup until smooth. Stir in the cream, if using, and season with salt and pepper. Serve hot.

Zuppa di Cavolo Nero (Kale Soup)

Ingredients:

- 1 bunch kale, chopped
- 1 onion, chopped
- 2 carrots, chopped
- 2 celery stalks, chopped
- 2 garlic cloves, minced
- 4 cups vegetable broth
- 1 can white beans, drained and rinsed
- 1 tbsp olive oil
- Salt and pepper to taste

Instructions: Heat olive oil in a large pot over medium heat. Add the onion, carrots, celery, and garlic. Cook for about 8 minutes, until the vegetables begin to soften. Add the kale, vegetable broth, and white beans. Bring to a boil, then reduce to a simmer and cook for 30 minutes. Season with salt and pepper. Serve hot.

Risotto alla Milanese

Ingredients:

- 1 cup Arborio rice
- 4 cups chicken or vegetable broth
- 1 small onion, chopped
- 2 tbsp butter
- 1 tbsp olive oil
- 1/4 tsp saffron threads
- 1/4 cup dry white wine
- 1/2 cup grated Parmesan cheese
- Salt and pepper to taste

Instructions: In a small bowl, steep the saffron threads in a little hot broth for about 10 minutes. In a large pan, heat the olive oil and butter over medium heat. Add the onion and cook until softened, about 5 minutes. Add the Arborio rice and stir to coat the rice in the butter. Pour in the white wine and cook until it evaporates. Gradually add the warm broth, one ladle at a time, stirring constantly and allowing the liquid to absorb before adding more. When the rice is tender and creamy, stir in the saffron-infused broth and Parmesan cheese. Season with salt and pepper and serve hot.

Risotto ai Funghi (Mushroom Risotto)

Ingredients:

- 1 cup Arborio rice
- 4 cups vegetable broth
- 1/2 lb mushrooms, sliced (preferably a mix of wild mushrooms)
- 1 small onion, chopped
- 2 tbsp butter
- 1 tbsp olive oil
- 1/4 cup dry white wine
- 1/2 cup grated Parmesan cheese
- Salt and pepper to taste

Instructions: Heat olive oil and 1 tbsp butter in a large pan over medium heat. Add the onion and cook for about 5 minutes. Add the mushrooms and cook until they release their moisture and become soft, about 8 minutes. Add the Arborio rice and stir for 1-2 minutes. Pour in the white wine and cook until evaporated. Gradually add the warm vegetable broth, stirring constantly until the liquid is absorbed before adding more. Continue this process until the rice is creamy and cooked al dente, about 20 minutes. Stir in the remaining butter and Parmesan cheese. Season with salt and pepper and serve hot.

Risotto alla Pescatora (Seafood Risotto)

Ingredients:

- 1 cup Arborio rice
- 4 cups fish stock or water
- 1 lb mixed seafood (shrimp, mussels, clams, squid)
- 1 small onion, chopped
- 2 tbsp olive oil
- 1/4 cup dry white wine
- 1/2 cup grated Parmesan cheese
- Fresh parsley for garnish
- Salt and pepper to taste

Instructions: In a large pan, heat olive oil over medium heat. Add the onion and cook for 5 minutes until softened. Add the Arborio rice and stir to coat with oil. Pour in the white wine and cook until it evaporates. Gradually add the warm fish stock, one ladle at a time, stirring constantly. Once the rice is halfway cooked, add the mixed seafood. Continue cooking until the rice is creamy and the seafood is cooked through, about 15-20 minutes. Stir in the Parmesan cheese and season with salt and pepper. Garnish with fresh parsley and serve immediately.

Risotto alla Carbonara

Ingredients:

- 1 cup Arborio rice
- 4 cups chicken broth
- 1 small onion, chopped
- 2 tbsp olive oil
- 1/2 cup pancetta or guanciale, diced
- 2 large eggs
- 1/2 cup grated Pecorino Romano cheese
- Salt and pepper to taste

Instructions: In a pan, heat olive oil over medium heat. Add the diced pancetta and cook until crispy, about 5 minutes. Remove from heat and set aside. In a separate pan, heat the chicken broth and keep warm. Add the chopped onion to the pan and sauté for 5 minutes until softened. Add the Arborio rice and stir to coat with oil. Gradually add the warm chicken broth, one ladle at a time, stirring constantly. Once the rice is cooked, remove from heat and stir in the pancetta. In a bowl, whisk the eggs with the Pecorino Romano. Pour the egg mixture into the rice, stirring quickly to prevent the eggs from scrambling. Season with salt and pepper and serve hot.

Risotto al Nero di Seppia (Squid Ink Risotto)

Ingredients:

- 1 cup Arborio rice
- 4 cups fish stock or water
- 1 small onion, chopped
- 2 tbsp olive oil
- 1/4 cup dry white wine
- 1/2 lb squid, cleaned and sliced
- 2 tbsp squid ink
- 1/2 cup grated Parmesan cheese
- Salt and pepper to taste

Instructions: In a large pan, heat olive oil over medium heat. Add the onion and cook until softened, about 5 minutes. Add the Arborio rice and stir to coat in the oil. Pour in the white wine and cook until it evaporates. Gradually add the warm fish stock, one ladle at a time, stirring constantly. When the rice is almost cooked, add the sliced squid and squid ink. Stir until the ink colors the rice black and the squid is tender, about 5 minutes. Stir in the Parmesan cheese and season with salt and pepper. Serve hot.

Zuppa di Cipolle (Onion Soup)

Ingredients:

- 4 large onions, thinly sliced
- 2 tbsp butter
- 1 tbsp olive oil
- 4 cups beef or vegetable broth
- 1/4 cup dry white wine
- 1 tsp thyme
- 1 bay leaf
- Salt and pepper to taste
- 4 slices baguette
- 1 cup grated Gruyère or Parmesan cheese

Instructions: In a large pot, heat the butter and olive oil over medium heat. Add the onions and cook, stirring occasionally, until softened and caramelized, about 25 minutes. Add the white wine and cook for another 2 minutes. Stir in the broth, thyme, bay leaf, salt, and pepper. Bring to a boil, then reduce the heat and simmer for 20 minutes. While the soup is simmering, toast the baguette slices. Ladle the soup into bowls, top with a slice of toasted bread, and sprinkle with grated cheese. Broil for 2-3 minutes until the cheese is melted and golden. Serve hot.

Zuppa di Asparagi (Asparagus Soup)

Ingredients:

- 1 lb fresh asparagus, trimmed and chopped
- 1 onion, chopped
- 2 tbsp olive oil
- 4 cups vegetable or chicken broth
- 1/2 cup cream (optional)
- Salt and pepper to taste
- Fresh parsley for garnish

Instructions: In a large pot, heat olive oil over medium heat. Add the chopped onion and cook until softened, about 5 minutes. Add the asparagus and cook for 5 minutes. Pour in the broth and bring to a boil. Reduce the heat and simmer for 20 minutes, until the asparagus is tender. Using an immersion blender, puree the soup until smooth. Stir in the cream (if using) and season with salt and pepper. Garnish with fresh parsley and serve hot.

Crema di Pomodoro (Tomato Cream Soup)

Ingredients:

- 6 large tomatoes, peeled and chopped
- 1 onion, chopped
- 2 garlic cloves, minced
- 2 tbsp olive oil
- 4 cups vegetable or chicken broth
- 1/2 cup heavy cream
- Salt and pepper to taste
- Fresh basil for garnish

Instructions: Heat olive oil in a large pot over medium heat. Add the onion and garlic, and cook until softened, about 5 minutes. Add the chopped tomatoes and cook for another 5 minutes. Pour in the broth and bring to a simmer. Cook for 20 minutes. Use an immersion blender to puree the soup until smooth. Stir in the cream and season with salt and pepper. Garnish with fresh basil and serve hot.

Sformato di Melanzane (Eggplant Flan)

Ingredients:

- 2 medium eggplants, peeled and cubed
- 1 cup ricotta cheese
- 1/2 cup grated Parmesan cheese
- 2 eggs
- 2 tbsp olive oil
- Salt and pepper to taste
- Fresh basil for garnish

Instructions: Preheat the oven to 375°F (190°C). Heat olive oil in a pan over medium heat, add the eggplant cubes, and sauté until soft, about 10 minutes. In a bowl, combine the ricotta, Parmesan, eggs, salt, and pepper. Mash the cooked eggplant and add it to the ricotta mixture. Stir to combine. Pour the mixture into a greased baking dish and bake for 30 minutes, or until golden on top. Let cool slightly before serving, and garnish with fresh basil.

Purè di Patate (Mashed Potatoes)

Ingredients:

- 2 lbs potatoes, peeled and cubed
- 1/2 cup butter
- 1/2 cup milk
- Salt and pepper to taste

Instructions: Place the potatoes in a pot of salted water and bring to a boil. Cook for 15-20 minutes until tender. Drain the potatoes and return them to the pot. Mash the potatoes with a potato masher or hand mixer. Add the butter and milk, and continue to mash until smooth and creamy. Season with salt and pepper. Serve hot.

Trippa alla Romana

Ingredients:

- 2 lbs tripe, cleaned and cut into strips
- 2 tbsp olive oil
- 1 onion, chopped
- 2 garlic cloves, minced
- 1 can (14 oz) diced tomatoes
- 2 tbsp tomato paste
- 1/2 cup dry white wine
- 1/2 cup grated Pecorino Romano cheese
- Salt and pepper to taste
- Fresh parsley for garnish

Instructions: In a large pot, heat olive oil over medium heat. Add the onion and garlic, and cook until softened, about 5 minutes. Add the tripe and cook for another 5 minutes. Stir in the tomatoes, tomato paste, and white wine, and bring to a simmer. Cook for 1 to 1.5 hours, stirring occasionally, until the tripe is tender. Season with salt and pepper. Serve with a generous sprinkle of Pecorino Romano and fresh parsley.

Polenta con Funghi (Polenta with Mushrooms)

Ingredients:

- 1 cup cornmeal (for polenta)
- 4 cups water
- 1/2 lb mixed mushrooms, sliced
- 2 tbsp olive oil
- 1/4 cup grated Parmesan cheese
- Salt and pepper to taste

Instructions: Bring the water to a boil in a pot, and gradually add the cornmeal, stirring constantly. Lower the heat and cook, stirring frequently, for about 30 minutes, until the polenta is thick and creamy. While the polenta cooks, heat olive oil in a skillet over medium heat and sauté the mushrooms until tender, about 5 minutes. Season with salt and pepper. Serve the polenta topped with the sautéed mushrooms and a sprinkle of Parmesan cheese.

Polenta con Cinghiale (Polenta with Wild Boar)

Ingredients:

- 1 cup cornmeal (for polenta)
- 4 cups water
- 1 lb wild boar stew meat, cubed
- 2 tbsp olive oil
- 1 onion, chopped
- 2 garlic cloves, minced
- 1 cup red wine
- 2 cups beef broth
- 1 can (14 oz) diced tomatoes
- Salt and pepper to taste
- Fresh rosemary for garnish

Instructions: To make the polenta, bring the water to a boil, and gradually add the cornmeal, stirring constantly. Lower the heat and cook, stirring frequently, for about 30 minutes, until thick and creamy. For the wild boar, heat olive oil in a large pan over medium heat. Add the boar meat and brown on all sides. Remove the meat and set aside. In the same pan, sauté the onion and garlic until softened. Add the wine, beef broth, and tomatoes. Return the boar to the pan, and simmer for 1.5 to 2 hours, until the meat is tender. Serve the wild boar on top of the polenta, garnished with fresh rosemary.

Fagioli all'Uccelletto

Ingredients:

- 2 cups dried cannellini beans, soaked overnight
- 2 tbsp olive oil
- 1 onion, chopped
- 2 garlic cloves, minced
- 1 can (14 oz) diced tomatoes
- 2 tsp fresh sage, chopped
- Salt and pepper to taste

Instructions: Drain and rinse the soaked beans. In a large pot, heat olive oil over medium heat. Add the onion and garlic, and cook until softened. Stir in the tomatoes, beans, sage, salt, and pepper. Add enough water to cover the beans, and bring to a boil. Lower the heat and simmer for 1-1.5 hours, until the beans are tender. Serve hot, drizzled with olive oil.

Parmigiana di Melanzane (Eggplant Parmesan)

Ingredients:

- 2 large eggplants, sliced into 1/4-inch rounds
- 2 cups marinara sauce
- 2 cups mozzarella cheese, shredded
- 1/2 cup grated Parmesan cheese
- 1/4 cup fresh basil, chopped
- Olive oil for frying
- Salt and pepper to taste

Instructions: Preheat the oven to 375°F (190°C). Sprinkle the eggplant slices with salt and let them sit for 30 minutes to draw out excess moisture. Pat dry with paper towels. In a large skillet, heat olive oil over medium heat and fry the eggplant slices until golden brown on both sides. Drain on paper towels. In a baking dish, layer the fried eggplant slices with marinara sauce, mozzarella, Parmesan, and basil. Repeat the layers until all the ingredients are used. Bake for 30 minutes, until the cheese is bubbly and golden. Serve hot.

Gnocchi alla Romana

Ingredients:

- 1 1/2 cups semolina flour
- 4 cups milk
- 1/4 cup butter
- 1/2 cup grated Parmesan cheese
- 2 large egg yolks
- Salt and pepper to taste
- Butter for greasing the baking dish

Instructions: Preheat the oven to 375°F (190°C). In a saucepan, bring the milk to a simmer with a pinch of salt. Gradually add the semolina flour while whisking constantly to prevent lumps. Cook for about 10-12 minutes, stirring constantly until the mixture thickens. Remove from the heat and stir in the butter, Parmesan cheese, egg yolks, salt, and pepper. Spread the mixture onto a greased baking sheet or dish, smoothing it into an even layer. Once it cools, cut the dough into discs or squares. Arrange the gnocchi in a buttered baking dish, sprinkle with additional Parmesan, and bake for 20 minutes until golden brown. Serve hot.

Risotto al Gorgonzola

Ingredients:

- 1 cup Arborio rice
- 4 cups chicken or vegetable broth
- 1 small onion, chopped
- 2 tbsp butter
- 1/4 cup white wine
- 1/2 cup Gorgonzola cheese, crumbled
- 1/4 cup heavy cream
- Salt and pepper to taste
- Fresh parsley for garnish

Instructions: In a large pan, heat butter over medium heat. Add the onion and cook until softened, about 5 minutes. Add the rice and stir to coat. Pour in the white wine and let it evaporate. Gradually add the warm broth, one ladle at a time, stirring constantly until the rice absorbs the liquid. Continue until the rice is creamy and al dente, about 18-20 minutes. Stir in the Gorgonzola cheese and heavy cream, and season with salt and pepper. Garnish with fresh parsley and serve immediately.

Tortino di Riso (Rice Cake)

Ingredients:

- 2 cups cooked rice (preferably day-old rice)
- 1/2 cup grated Parmesan cheese
- 2 eggs, beaten
- 1/4 cup butter, melted
- 1/2 cup breadcrumbs
- Salt and pepper to taste
- Fresh parsley for garnish

Instructions: Preheat the oven to 375°F (190°C). In a large bowl, combine the cooked rice, Parmesan cheese, beaten eggs, melted butter, breadcrumbs, salt, and pepper. Mix well to combine. Grease a baking dish and spoon the rice mixture into the dish, pressing it down gently. Bake for 25-30 minutes, or until golden and crisp on top. Garnish with fresh parsley and serve hot.

Pasticcio di Carne

Ingredients:

- 1 lb ground beef
- 1 onion, chopped
- 2 garlic cloves, minced
- 1/2 cup red wine
- 1 can (14 oz) crushed tomatoes
- 1/2 cup heavy cream
- 1/2 cup grated Parmesan cheese
- 2 tbsp butter
- Salt and pepper to taste
- 1 sheet puff pastry

Instructions: Preheat the oven to 375°F (190°C). In a large skillet, melt butter over medium heat and sauté the onion and garlic until softened. Add the ground beef and cook until browned. Pour in the red wine and let it simmer for 5 minutes. Stir in the crushed tomatoes, heavy cream, Parmesan, salt, and pepper. Simmer for 20 minutes, stirring occasionally, until the mixture thickens. Roll out the puff pastry on a lightly floured surface. Spoon the meat mixture onto the pastry and fold it over to create a parcel. Bake for 30 minutes, or until the pastry is golden and crisp. Serve hot.

Insalata Caprese (Caprese Salad)

Ingredients:

- 3 ripe tomatoes, sliced
- 8 oz fresh mozzarella cheese, sliced
- Fresh basil leaves
- 1 tbsp olive oil
- 1 tbsp balsamic vinegar
- Salt and pepper to taste

Instructions: Arrange the sliced tomatoes and mozzarella on a serving platter, alternating between the two. Tuck fresh basil leaves between the slices. Drizzle with olive oil and balsamic vinegar, and season with salt and pepper. Serve immediately as a light appetizer or side dish.

Cannoli Siciliani (Sicilian Pastry)

Ingredients for the Shells:

- 2 cups all-purpose flour
- 1/4 cup sugar
- 1/4 tsp cinnamon
- 1/4 tsp cocoa powder
- 1/4 cup cold butter
- 1/4 cup white wine
- 1 egg, beaten
- Vegetable oil for frying

Ingredients for the Filling:

- 1 1/2 cups ricotta cheese, drained
- 1/2 cup powdered sugar
- 1/2 tsp vanilla extract
- 1/4 cup chocolate chips
- Crushed pistachios for garnish (optional)

Instructions: To make the shells, combine the flour, sugar, cinnamon, and cocoa powder in a bowl. Cut in the cold butter until the mixture resembles breadcrumbs. Add the wine and beaten egg, and mix until a dough forms. Wrap the dough in plastic wrap and refrigerate for 30 minutes. Roll out the dough to 1/8-inch thickness and cut into circles. Wrap the dough around metal cannoli tubes and seal the edges with a little water. Heat oil in a deep fryer or large pot to 350°F (175°C) and fry the cannoli shells until golden and crispy, about 3-4 minutes. Drain on paper towels and let cool.

For the filling, combine the ricotta, powdered sugar, and vanilla extract in a bowl. Stir in the chocolate chips. Once the shells have cooled, carefully remove the tubes and fill each shell with the ricotta mixture. Garnish with crushed pistachios and serve immediately.

Tiramisu

Ingredients:

- 1 1/2 cups strong brewed coffee, cooled
- 1/4 cup coffee liqueur (optional)
- 3 large egg yolks
- 1/2 cup sugar
- 1 cup mascarpone cheese
- 1 cup heavy cream
- 1 tsp vanilla extract
- 24 ladyfingers
- Unsweetened cocoa powder, for dusting
- Dark chocolate shavings (optional)

Instructions: In a shallow dish, combine the coffee and coffee liqueur. In a large bowl, whisk the egg yolks and sugar together until thick and pale. Stir in the mascarpone cheese until smooth. In a separate bowl, whip the heavy cream and vanilla extract until soft peaks form. Gently fold the whipped cream into the mascarpone mixture.

Dip the ladyfingers into the coffee mixture for a second or two (do not soak them) and layer them at the bottom of a serving dish. Spread half of the mascarpone mixture over the ladyfingers. Repeat the layers, ending with the mascarpone mixture on top. Cover and refrigerate for at least 4 hours, preferably overnight. Before serving, dust with cocoa powder and garnish with chocolate shavings, if desired.

Panna Cotta

Ingredients:

- 1 1/2 cups heavy cream
- 1/2 cup whole milk
- 1/2 cup sugar
- 1 tsp vanilla extract
- 1 packet (1 tsp) unflavored gelatin
- Fresh berries or fruit compote for garnish (optional)

Instructions: In a small bowl, sprinkle the gelatin over 2 tbsp of cold milk and let it sit for 5 minutes. In a saucepan, combine the cream, milk, and sugar. Heat over medium heat, stirring occasionally, until the sugar is dissolved and the mixture is hot but not boiling. Remove from heat and stir in the vanilla extract. Add the gelatin mixture to the hot cream mixture and stir until the gelatin is completely dissolved.

Pour the mixture into individual ramekins or molds. Let cool to room temperature, then refrigerate for at least 4 hours or overnight until set. Before serving, top with fresh berries or fruit compote, if desired.

Cassata Siciliana

Ingredients for the Cake:

- 1 1/2 cups all-purpose flour
- 1 cup sugar
- 4 large eggs
- 1/2 cup unsalted butter, melted
- 1 tsp vanilla extract
- 1/2 tsp baking powder
- 1/4 tsp salt

Ingredients for the Filling:

- 1 1/2 cups ricotta cheese, drained
- 1/2 cup powdered sugar
- 1 tsp vanilla extract
- 1/4 cup candied orange peel, chopped
- 1/4 cup chocolate chips
- 1/4 cup maraschino cherries, chopped

Ingredients for the Decoration:

- 1/2 cup fondant or marzipan, rolled thin
- 1 tbsp powdered sugar (for dusting)

Instructions: Preheat the oven to 350°F (175°C). Grease and flour a round cake pan. In a bowl, beat the eggs and sugar until pale and fluffy. Stir in the melted butter and vanilla extract. Sift the flour, baking powder, and salt, and fold them into the egg mixture. Pour the batter into the prepared cake pan and bake for 25-30 minutes, or until a toothpick comes out clean. Let the cake cool completely.

For the filling, combine the ricotta cheese, powdered sugar, vanilla, candied orange peel, chocolate chips, and maraschino cherries in a bowl. Once the cake has cooled, slice it into two layers. Spread the ricotta mixture between the layers, then cover the entire cake with fondant or marzipan. Dust with powdered sugar and refrigerate before serving.

Sformato di Ricotta (Ricotta Flan)

Ingredients:

- 2 cups ricotta cheese
- 2 eggs
- 1/2 cup heavy cream
- 1/4 cup grated Parmesan cheese
- 1 tbsp fresh parsley, chopped
- Salt and pepper to taste
- Butter for greasing the baking dish

Instructions: Preheat the oven to 375°F (190°C). Grease a baking dish with butter. In a large bowl, whisk together the ricotta cheese, eggs, heavy cream, Parmesan, parsley, salt, and pepper until smooth. Pour the mixture into the prepared dish and smooth the top.

Bake for 30-35 minutes, or until the flan is golden on top and set in the center. Let cool for 10 minutes before serving. Serve warm or at room temperature.

Zuppa di Zucca (Pumpkin Soup)

Ingredients:

- 2 lbs pumpkin, peeled and cubed
- 1 onion, chopped
- 2 garlic cloves, minced
- 4 cups vegetable broth
- 1/2 cup heavy cream
- 2 tbsp olive oil
- Salt and pepper to taste
- Fresh thyme or parsley for garnish

Instructions: In a large pot, heat olive oil over medium heat. Add the onion and garlic and cook until softened, about 5 minutes. Add the pumpkin and cook for an additional 5 minutes. Pour in the vegetable broth and bring to a boil. Reduce the heat and simmer for 20 minutes, or until the pumpkin is tender.

Use an immersion blender or transfer the soup to a blender and puree until smooth. Return the soup to the pot and stir in the heavy cream. Season with salt and pepper. Garnish with fresh thyme or parsley before serving.

Focaccia al Rosmarino (Rosemary Focaccia)

Ingredients:

- 3 cups all-purpose flour
- 1 packet (2 1/4 tsp) active dry yeast
- 1 cup warm water
- 1/4 cup olive oil, plus extra for drizzling
- 1 tbsp fresh rosemary, chopped
- 1 tsp salt
- 1 tbsp sugar

Instructions: In a bowl, combine the warm water, sugar, and yeast. Let it sit for about 10 minutes until it becomes foamy. Add the flour, olive oil, and salt to the yeast mixture and stir to form a dough. Knead the dough for 5-7 minutes until smooth and elastic. Cover the dough and let it rise in a warm place for about 1 hour or until doubled in size.

Preheat the oven to 400°F (200°C). Punch down the dough and spread it out on a greased baking sheet. Use your fingers to create dimples in the dough. Drizzle with olive oil, sprinkle with rosemary, and season with salt. Bake for 20-25 minutes, or until golden brown. Serve warm.

www.ingramcontent.com/pod-product-compliance
Lightning Source LLC
LaVergne TN
LVHW081340060526
838201LV00055B/2756